Female FOODIES

Ruth Fertel

Ruth's Chris Steak House Creator

Rebecca Felix

Checkerboard Library

An Imprint of Abdo Publishing
abdopublishing.com

abdopublishing.com

Published by Abdo Publishing, a division of ABDO, PO Box 398166, Minneapolis, Minnesota 55439. Copyright © 2018 by Abdo Consulting Group, Inc. International copyrights reserved in all countries. No part of this book may be reproduced in any form without written permission from the publisher. Checkerboard Library™ is a trademark and logo of Abdo Publishing.

Printed in the United States of America, North Mankato, Minnesota
102017
012018

THIS BOOK CONTAINS
RECYCLED MATERIALS

Design: Sarah DeYoung, Mighty Media, Inc.
Production: Mighty Media, Inc.
Editor: Liz Salzmann
Cover Photographs: Photo courtesy of Ruth's Chris Steak House, Randy Fertel
Interior Photographs: Alamy, p. 21; Florida Keys Public Libraries/Flickr, p. 17; Randy Fertel, pp. 5, 7, 9, 11, 13, 15, 19, 25, 28 (top, bottom), 29 (top, bottom); Shutterstock, pp. 3, 5, 7, 9, 11, 13, 15, 17, 19, 21, 23, 25, 31
Background Pattern: Shutterstock, cover, pp. 3, 5, 7, 9, 11, 13, 15, 17, 19, 21, 23, 25, 31

Publisher's Cataloging-in-Publication Data
Names: Felix, Rebecca, author.
Title: Ruth Fertel: Ruth's Chris Steak House creator / by Rebecca Felix.
Other titles: Ruth's Chris Steak House creator
Description: Minneapolis, Minnesota : Abdo Publishing, 2018. | Series: Female foodies |
    Includes online resources and index.
Identifiers: LCCN 2017944040 | ISBN 9781532112676 (lib.bdg.) | ISBN 9781532150395 (ebook)
Subjects: LCSH: Fertel, Ruth, 1927-2002.--Juvenile literature. | Businesswomen--United States--
    Biography--Juvenile literature. | Restaurateurs--Juvenile literature. | Entrepreneurship--Juvenile
    literature.
Classification: DDC 338.76647 [B]--dc23
LC record available at https://lccn.loc.gov/2017944040

Contents

Chapter 1

Empress of Steak

It's Saturday night, and a special occasion. Your family is celebrating your parents' **anniversary** at a steak house. As you're seated in a sleek leather booth, you hear a **sizzle** start soft and grow louder.

A server carries a giant slab of meat past your table. Butter is bubbling on the steak's surface. This is Ruth's Chris Steak House's **signature** touch. The scent hits you next. Your mouth waters for your own steak!

Ruth Fertel is the founder of Ruth's Chris Steak House. It is a national **chain** known for quality, sizzling steaks. Fertel opened her first steak house in 1965. Today, there are more than 150 steak houses bearing her name around the world.

Fertel was a self-taught restaurant owner, cook, and businesswoman. She became such an expert on quality beef that she was often called the "Empress of Steak." Fertel took big risks and saw big success. Her desire to succeed began at a young age, in a small Louisiana schoolhouse.

Ruth Fertel in the early 1950s

Chapter 2

Early Achievements

Ruth Ann Udstad was born on February 5, 1927, in New Orleans, Louisiana. Ruth's family lived in the nearby town of Happy Jack. Ruth's father was an insurance salesman. Her mother was a teacher.

Several of Ruth's family members were great cooks. They also liked to hunt and fish. Ruth loved to hunt and fish too. She was also very competitive, especially with her brother, Sig. Sig was three years older than Ruth, but Ruth tried to beat him at anything she could. This included at school.

Ruth and Sig attended nearby Port Sulphur's Rigaud Elementary School. It was a one-room schoolhouse. All grades were taught in one room. Ruth advanced in her studies by listening to what the teachers were teaching the older students. She learned enough this way that she was moved ahead two grades!

Food Bite

Ruth loved to ride horses and read. She was also very good at solving puzzles.

Ruth (*left*) and Sig with their father, Arthur Simpson Udstad

Finishing grade school early meant Ruth finished high school early too. She graduated in 1942 at the age of 15. She went on to college at Louisiana State University in Baton Rouge. She graduated with degrees in physics and chemistry in 1946.

Chapter 3

Family and Horses

For a short time after college, Udstad was a science teacher. She taught at John McNeese Junior College in Lake Charles, Louisiana. Around this time, Udstad met a man named Rodney Fertel. The two began dating and married in 1947. Udstad changed her last name to Fertel.

Fertel quit her teaching job and moved to New Orleans, Louisiana, where Rodney was raised. Fertel and Rodney both had a passion for horses. They enjoyed riding and owning the animals. But they especially enjoyed betting on horse racing.

In 1951, the couple opened a horse stable. Fertel learned to train the racehorses. In 1955, she became the first woman in Louisiana licensed to train **Thoroughbred** horses.

The Fertels had two sons together, Jerry and Randy. For many years, Fertel focused on raising her children and taking care of the family's home. In 1958, Fertel and Rodney separated. After that, Rodney was in his sons' lives on and off. Fertel was responsible for their well-being and finances full time.

The Fertels often vacationed in Hot Springs, Arkansas.

Chapter 4

A Big Idea

Fertel was now a single mom. She needed to earn money to support herself and her sons. So, she took on odd jobs, including sewing. Fertel sewed curtains in her home and then hung them in her customers' windows.

In addition, Fertel worked as a lab technician at Tulane Medical School in New Orleans. However, Fertel's lab job still didn't pay as much money as she hoped. She wanted to earn enough to send her sons to college.

Fertel kept her job, but continued to look for other opportunities. She soon came across an ad in a local newspaper. It stated that an "established steak house" was for sale. The ad didn't include the name of the restaurant, only the address. It turned out to be Chris Steak House. Fertel was familiar with the restaurant, as she had eaten there with her family.

But Fertel had never worked in the food industry. Still, the idea of owning a restaurant appealed to her. She believed it was something she could do, experienced or not. It was the start of her famous steak house history.

Fertel and her sons, Randy (*left*) and Jerry, during a visit to Happy Jack

Chapter 5

Ignoring Naysayers

The ad wasn't the only thing that convinced Fertel to buy Chris Steak House. After becoming interested, she visited the site and spoke to the current owner, Chris Matulich. As the two spoke, Matulich told Fertel the restaurant had been established on February 5, 1927. That was Fertel's birth date! She felt this was a good **omen**, and committed to buying the restaurant.

Fertel was possibly the only person who felt good about her decision. Her friends and family thought she was crazy. Fertel's brother, Sig, owned a restaurant in Happy Jack. He knew it was hard work, even for experienced owners.

Bankers also thought Fertel's idea was a bad one. She **mortgaged** her house to raise the money to buy Chris Steak House. But the banker pointed out that Fertel would need several thousand

Food Bite

Both Randy and Jerry worked for their mom's restaurant **chain** at some point in their lives.

Fertel's determination helped her achieve great success in both horse training and business!

dollars more to stock the restaurant. Fertel agreed and asked to borrow $4,000 more. The banker gave her the additional money.

Fertel didn't let other people's opinions stop her. In fact, her son Randy thought they had the opposite effect! He felt people telling her she couldn't succeed inspired her to do just that.

Chapter 6

Setting Up Shop

Fertel took ownership of Chris Steak House in May 1965. She kept the restaurant's name so it would remain familiar to old customers. Matulich also told Fertel he would stick around to teach her to run the restaurant. But after the sale, he emptied the cash register and never returned.

Fertel followed her instincts in teaching herself every aspect of the business. Fertel knew that Matulich had butchered the meat himself, so she learned how to do it too. It was hard work. Fertel often had small cuts on her arms from the saw.

When helping the kitchen staff during business hours, Fertel left the door open a bit. She wanted her customers to see how hard she was working. Fertel felt that would make them want her to succeed.

Fertel used this same method in the front of the house. Her desk was right in the restaurant, near the bar and front door. This way, diners could see her taking care of her business. Fertel's hard work and methods paid off. The steak house stayed busy and earned new customers.

In addition to managing the restaurant, Fertel often helped out as hostess, waitress, and cook.

Chapter 7

Close Calls

Chris Steak House did well for the first few months. However, four months after opening, **disaster** struck. **Hurricane** Betsy hit New Orleans in September 1965. The storm caused flooding and power outages across the city.

Chris Steak House wasn't damaged by the storm, but it lost power. Even though Fertel's gas broilers still worked, the restaurant's lights and refrigerators did not. She was forced to close.

Knowing the food would spoil without refrigeration, Fertel cooked it all. She offered free meals to first responders and workers repairing the storm damage. Her generosity did not go unnoticed. When Chris Steak House reopened, business boomed.

Chris Steak House ran smoothly for several more years. Then, in 1971, Fertel faced danger again. She came face-to-face with a robber.

Food Bite

Fertel was a risk-taker. In the 1960s, she learned to fly a single-engine airplane.

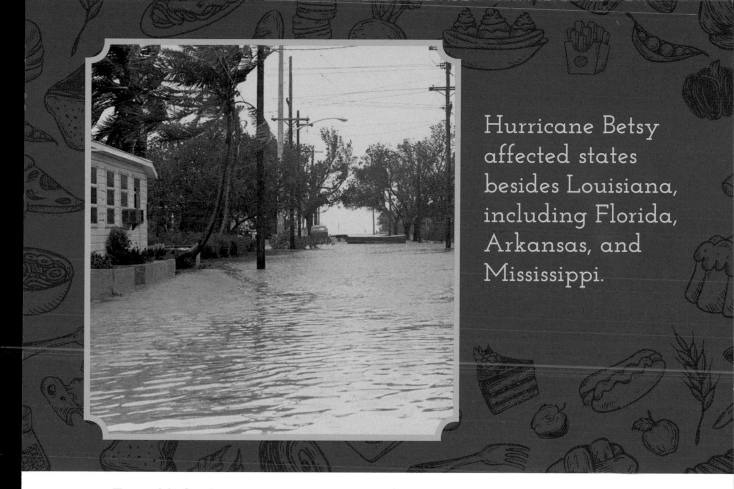

Hurricane Betsy affected states besides Louisiana, including Florida, Arkansas, and Mississippi.

Fertel left the restaurant one night with the day's earnings in her purse. A man approached her and grabbed her purse. Fertel wouldn't let go. The man shot her in the shoulder. Still, she kept her grip. The robber then ran away.

Fertel healed and got right back to work. She refused to move locations. Instead, she bought a shotgun and kept it at the restaurant. She also hired an off-duty police officer to provide security outside the building.

Chapter 8

Reborn Ruth's Chris

Fertel had been through a lot during her first ten years of business. Remaining standing after a **hurricane** and robbery were no small feats. But in 1976, a third **disaster** brought the end of Chris Steak House.

At the time, people often smoked cigarettes indoors, including in restaurants. Each night, Chris Steak House employees dumped the ashes onto the dirty tablecloths, which were then piled up to be washed. One night, one of the cigarettes hadn't been completely put out. The cigarette caught the tablecloths on fire, and then the restaurant.

The kitchen burned down and the dining room was badly damaged from smoke. But Fertel wasn't ready to let the fire end her business. She moved her restaurant to a building four blocks away.

Fertel hired construction workers to turn the building into a restaurant. Within just one week, it was ready to open! However, there was one problem. Fertel's contract to buy Chris Steak House only allowed her to use the name at

Chris Steak House customers included working-class people, families, and even politicians!

the original location. But Fertel didn't want to change the name completely. Customers had come to associate it with great steaks, and with her. So, Fertel simply changed the restaurant name by adding hers to it. Ruth's Chris Steak House was born!

Chapter 9

Special Sizzle

Fertel's steak house had a new name but served the same great food. Each steak came with warm bread. The sides were purchased separately. They included potato dishes and salads.

Ruth's Chris Steak House was known for its generous portions. But the way Fertel served her steaks became the restaurant's **signature**. The steaks were cooked in special broilers. They broiled the steaks at 1,800 degrees Fahrenheit (982°C). This was much hotter than an average broiler. The high heat seared the outsides of the steaks, but left the insides tender and juicy.

The steaks were placed on plates heated to 500 degrees Fahrenheit (260°C). Then the steaming steaks were topped with butter that bubbled on contact. The butter created a mouthwatering **sizzling** sound on the way to the tables.

Food Bite

Fertel said, "The butter melts and mixes with the juice from the steak. Can you imagine anything tasting better?"

Fertel originally charged $5.50 for her steaks. This was expensive at the time, but Fertel believed people would pay for quality.

Lana Duke, Fertel's friend and business associate, used this **sizzle** to promote the steak house. Duke had a TV commercial made that showed a Ruth's Chris steak giving off a loud sizzle. The sound took the place of any spoken words. A line of text appeared on the screen. It read, "The Steak that Speaks for Itself." After the commercial began airing, the restaurant's attendance increased. Many customers talked about the ad.

Chapter 10

New Locations

Ruth's Chris **signature** steaks were a favorite with New Orleans diners. But not all Fertel's customers were local. Some traveled many miles just to eat at her restaurant.

One such customer was T.J. Moran. Moran often traveled roughly 90 miles (145 km) from Baton Rouge, Louisiana, to New Orleans just to eat a Ruth's Chris steak. He also often asked Fertel to open a location in his town. This request and Ruth's Chris success led Fertel to **franchise** her restaurant. Moran opened the first franchised Ruth's Chris Steak House in 1977.

The Baton Rouge location was the first of many franchised Ruth's Chris restaurants. In the following years, several more opened around the nation. Fertel traveled to every new opening. She would spend weeks on location to help get the new restaurant up and running.

Each new location had its own look and feel. This was a decision Fertel made. She wanted each restaurant to have a style that fit its location and customers. What tied them all together was the food and the name.

Ruth's Chris Steak House has spread far beyond Louisiana, including a store at Inner Harbor in Baltimore, Maryland.

Chapter 11

Inspiring Women

Ruth's Chris Steak House didn't just expand outside New Orleans. Fertel also opened additional locations in the restaurant's hometown. She often promoted her female servers or female friends to run these locations.

Female restaurant owners were not common when Fertel first entered the industry. When she bought Chris Steak House, many people were expecting her to fail because she was a woman. However, Fertel said, "I never had a doubt that I would make it."

Fertel worked to inspire this same **confidence** in the women around her. She sought to give women opportunities. As a single mother herself, Fertel especially wanted to help other single mothers. She felt they were the hardest workers. She hired as many single mothers as she could to work in her restaurants. This practice

Food Bite

In 1997, Fertel was named Executive of the Year by *Restaurants & Institutions* magazine.

One of Fertel's mottoes in life was, "Be yourself, unless you're no fun."

made Ruth's Chris unusual. At the time, most fine dining restaurants staffed only male servers.

Fertel knew she could count on single mothers to care about their jobs. They depended on the money they earned to raise their children, just as she had. Randy remembered that his mother's staff of single mothers was a big part of Ruth's Chris success. The women served customers quickly and professionally, but also with warmth.

Chapter 12

First Lady of Steak

Many of Fertel's staff members called her "Miss Ruth." Outside the restaurant, Fertel's peers also gave her nicknames. These included "First Lady of Steak" and "Empress of Steak."

The 1990s saw continued expansion of the restaurants. By 1998, there were 66 locations around the world. The next year, Fertel sold her ever-growing empire. Financial firm Madison Dearborn Partners bought the **chain**. The company promised to run the restaurants the way Fertel had.

In 2000, Fertel learned she had **cancer**. She died on April 16, 2002. She was buried in a **mausoleum** that has stained glass, sculptures, and many other fancy details. It leaves a lasting impression of the **confident**, joyful way Fertel lived.

Fertel's son Randy established the Ruth U. Fertel Foundation to support educational programs. Fertel's **legacy** also lives on in the more than 150 restaurants that bear her name. She turned one small restaurant into a successful steak house chain. Fertel's hard work and **zest** for life made her and her **sizzling** steaks famous worldwide.

Ruth Fertel
By the Numbers

7

days it took Fertel to open a new restaurant when Chris Steak House burned down

60

number of seats in Chris Steak House

30-40

weight in pounds (14-18 kg) of each beef slab Fertel would butcher by hand

90

percentage of sales that come from steaks in the Ruth's Chris **chain**

34

years Fertel owned and ran her restaurants

225,000,000

amount in dollars of sales Ruth's Chris restaurants made in 1998, the final year Fertel owned them

Timeline

1927

Ruth Ann Udstad is born on February 5 in New Orleans, Louisiana.

1942

Ruth graduates from high school at the age of 15.

1955

Fertel becomes the first woman in Louisiana to be a licensed Thoroughbred trainer.

1958

Fertel and Rodney separate. Fertel takes on sewing and lab technician work to support her sons.

1977

Fertel franchises her restaurant chain. The second location opens in Baton Rouge, Louisiana.

1946

Udstad graduates from Louisiana State University.

1947

Udstad marries Rodney Fertel and changes her name. The couple settles in New Orleans.

1965

Fertel buys Chris Steak House from Chris Matulich.

1976

Chris Steak House burns down. Fertel opens Ruth's Chris Steak House in a new building one week later.

1999

Fertel sells the Ruth's Chris Steak House chain to Madison Dearborn Partners.

2002

Fertel dies from cancer on April 16.

Glossary

anniversary – the date of a special event that is often celebrated each year.

cancer– any of a group of often deadly diseases marked by harmful changes in the normal growth of cells. Cancer can spread and destroy healthy tissues and organs.

chain – a group of businesses usually under a single ownership, management, or control.

confident – sure of oneself. Someone who is confident has confidence.

disaster – an event that causes damage, destruction, and often loss of life. Natural disasters include events such as hurricanes, tornadoes, and earthquakes.

franchise – to grant someone the right to sell a company's goods or services in a particular place.

hurricane – a tropical storm with winds of 74 miles per hour (119 kmh) or more. The winds circle around a calm center. Heavy rain and flooding are common.

legacy – something important or meaningful handed down from previous generations or from the past.

mausoleum – a large tomb that is usually stone and above ground.

mortgage (MAWR-gihj) – to borrow money equal to the value of property such as land or a house from a bank. The borrower pays back the money over a period of years.

omen – something that is believed to be a sign of a future event.

signature – something that sets apart or identifies an individual, group, or company.

sizzle – to make a hissing or sputtering noise in or as if in frying or burning. The sound is also called a sizzle.

Thoroughbred – an English breed of horses kept chiefly for racing.

zest – enjoyment, excitement, or energy.

Online Resources

Booklinks
NONFICTION
NETWORK
FREE! ONLINE NONFICTION RESOURCES

To learn more about Ruth Fertel, visit **abdobooklinks.com**. These links are routinely monitored and updated to provide the most current information available.

Index